THE OFFICIAL
WEST HAM UNITED
ANNUAL 2015

Written by Rob Pritchard
Designed by Jon Dalrymple

A Grange Publication

ISBN: 978-1-908925-75-6

£7.99

Contents

WEST HAM UNITED OFFICIAL ANNUAL 2015

THIS ANNUAL BELONGS TO:

....

MY AGE:

....

MY SCHOOL:

....

MY FOOTBALL TEAM:

....

MY POSITION:

....

MY FAVOURITE WEST HAM UNITED PLAYER:

....

WHERE WEST HAM UNITED WILL FINISH IN THE BARCLAYS PREMIER LEAGUE:

....

Mark Noble

A welcome message from Hammer of the Year Mark Noble

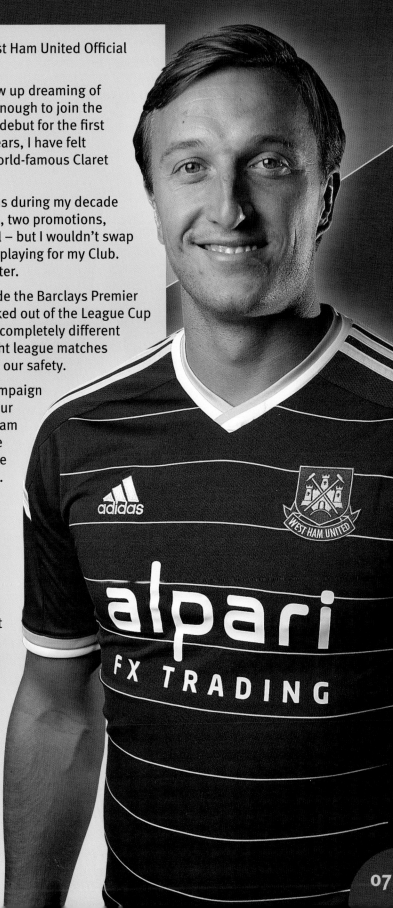

Hello everyone and welcome to the West Ham United Official Annual 2015.

Like you, I was born a Hammer and grew up dreaming of playing for the Club I love. I was lucky enough to join the Academy at the age of 13 and make my debut for the first team four years later. For the last ten years, I have felt pride and joy every time I pull on our world-famous Claret and Blue shirt.

I have experienced many ups and downs during my decade as a West Ham player – two relegations, two promotions, three Play-Off finals and an FA Cup final – but I wouldn't swap any of those experiences because I am playing for my Club. Last year, 2014, was another rollercoaster.

We began the year deep in trouble inside the Barclays Premier League relegation zone and were knocked out of the League Cup at the semi-final stage. February was a completely different matter, however, as we won four straight league matches to surge up the table and all but secure our safety.

The final few months of the 2013/14 campaign contained some highlights, including our third victory of the season over Tottenham Hotspur in our final home game, but we began this current season wanting to be more consistent and more entertaining.

Personally, I was honoured to win the Hammer of the Year and Players' Player of the Year awards in 2014. To receive the recognition of you, my fellow Hammers, for the second time was fantastic. If you'd told me I'd win Hammer of the Year once when I joined the Club as a 13-year-old kid, I wouldn't have believed you, so to win it twice is even more special. It was also great to win Players' Player of the Year because that was an endorsement of all the hard work I and my family put into my football every single day.

You all know how much I love playing for West Ham United and in front of the Claret and Blue Army, so long may our close relationship continue.

Come on you Irons!

Mark Noble

New Signings

Meet West Ham United's seven summer 2014 signings!

Aaron Cresswell

Carl Jenkinson

Cheikhou Kouyate

Diafra Sakho

Diego Poyet

Enner Valencia

Mauro Zarate

MARK Noble was crowned Hammer of the Year for a second time at the 2014 West Ham United Player Awards.

The midfielder completed a fine individual season by winning the fans' vote, with goalkeeper Adrian second and centre-back James Tomkins third.

A glittering evening, which raised tens of thousands of pounds for the Club's world-famous Academy, also saw graduate Sir Trevor Brooking presented with the second Lifetime Achievement Award.

Noble was also voted Players' Player of the Year by his squad-mates, while Adrian collected three awards – Signing of the Season, Save of the Season and Best Individual Performance.

Mark Noble was voted Players' Player of the Year

Captain Kevin Nolan finished as Top Goalscorer for the second straight season, while Ravel Morrison won the Goal of the Season prize for his outstanding individual strike in the 3-0 Barclays Premier League win at Tottenham Hotspur in October 2013.

That victory was also voted as the Team Performance of the Season.

The Academy's current stars were also honoured, with England U17 goalkeeper Sam Howes being named Young Hammer of the Year and Republic of Ireland U18 midfielder Josh Cullen winning the inaugural Dylan Tombides Award – named in honour of the late Australian forward, who died in April 2014 at the age of 20 following a courageous three-year battle with cancer.

Adrian left grasping a hat-trick of awards

Award Winners

Hammer of the Year
sponsored by Alpari FX
Mark Noble

Lifetime Achievement Award
sponsored by ACL
Sir Trevor Brooking

Signing of the Season
sponsored by S14 VIP Ltd
Adrian

Players' Player of the Year
sponsored by Asmatt
Mark Noble

Best Team Performance
sponsored by Call Print
**3-0 v Tottenham Hotspur (A),
Barclays Premier League**

Best Individual Performance
sponsored by Ark Build
**Adrian v Chelsea (A),
Barclays Premier League**

Top Goalscorer
sponsored by Mulalley
Kevin Nolan

Goal of the Season
sponsored by Lookers Range Rover Essex
Ravel Morrison

Save of the Season
sponsored by Higgins
**Adrian from Oscar v Chelsea (A),
Barclays Premier League**

Young Hammer of the Year
Sam Howes

Dylan Tombides Award
Josh Cullen

Kevin Nolan finished as Top Goalscorer for the second straight season

Josh Cullen was the inaugural winner of the Dylan Tombides Award

Sir Trevor Brooking received the Lifetime Achievement Award

New Stadium

West Ham United will move into their fantastic new home in Stratford in summer 2016

West Ham United have been granted the right to make the Olympic Stadium their home from the start of the 2016/17 season.

Here, you can see images of how the Stadium, already a prestigious part of the UK's sporting heritage, will be innovatively transformed into a world-class UEFA category 4, 54,000-seater venue fit to host the world's most famous competitions during the football season.

Developments will include the installation of a retractable seating solution on all four sides of the ground bringing fans closer to the action and the atmospheric, transparent roof that, at 84m, will become the largest-spanning tensile roof in the world.

West Ham United will move into the Stadium in summer 2016.

The Stadium will have a capacity of 54,000.

The Stadium will be a home fit for the Hammers.

The ambitious proposals also include first-class hospitality suites, the relocation inside the turnstile line of key facilities such as the concessions and toilets (as at other traditional football stadia), landscaping and a distinctive new building that is set to become the Hammers' exclusive Ticket Office and flagship Club Store.

The presence of these buildings will ensure that supporters continue to enjoy their direct relationship with the Club in new and enhanced facilities in the surroundings of the stunning Queen Elizabeth Olympic Park, which opened to the public in summer 2014.

The Club will continue to consult closely with supporters of all ages to help ensure the Stratford Stadium matches the high standards Hammers fans would expect from their new home.

Matt Jarvis and Carlton Cole paid a visit to the Queen Elizabeth Olympic Park.

The Hammer of the Year shows off his skills on the Stadium pitch.

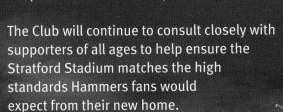

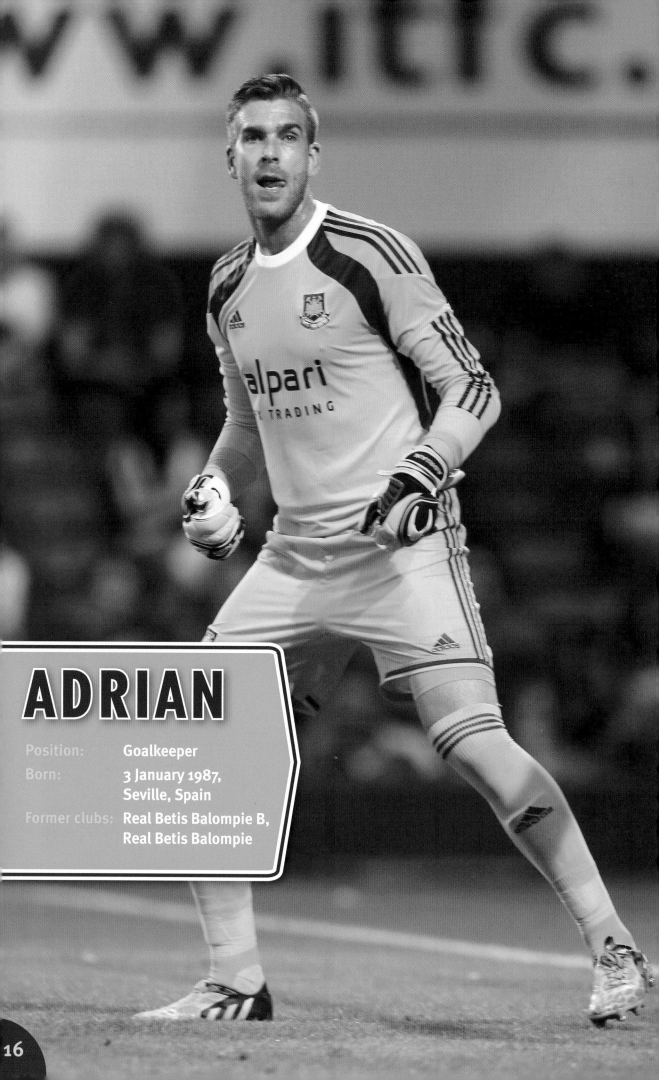

ADRIAN

Position: Goalkeeper

Born: 3 January 1987, Seville, Spain

Former clubs: Real Betis Balompie B, Real Betis Balompie

Manager: Sam Allardyce

Born: 19 October 1954, Dudley, England

Known universally as 'Big Sam', Dudley-born Sam Allardyce is one of the most experienced and respected managers in the English game.

A centre-back as a player, Big Sam forged his managerial reputation at Bolton Wanderers, who he led to four consecutive top-eight Premier League finishes, the League Cup final and into European football for the first time.

Big Sam led West Ham United to promotion to the Premier League in his first season with the Club.

Assistant manager: Neil McDonald

Born: 2 November 1965, Wallsend, England

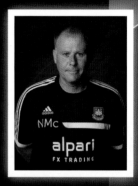

As a player, Neil McDonald was a reliable right-back or central midfielder who enjoyed success with Newcastle United and Everton.

Capped five times by England at U21 level, McDonald featured for the Toffees in their 1989 FA Cup final defeat by Liverpool at Wembley.

He served as Sam Allardyce's No2 at Bolton Wanderers and Blackburn Rovers before following Big Sam to West Ham United as his assistant in July 2011.

First-team coach: Ian Hendon

Born: 5 December 1971, Ilford, England

An FA Youth Cup winner with Tottenham Hotspur, Ian Hendon enjoyed a successful career as a centre-back with a variety of Football League clubs, captaining Sam Allardyce's Notts County to the Division Three title in 1998.

After managing Barnet and Dover Athletic, Hendon was reunited with Big Sam at West Ham United as U18s coach in July 2011 before being promoted to first-team coach in December 2012.

Goalkeeper coach: Martyn Margetson

Born: 8 September 1971, West Neath, Wales

Former Wales international goalkeeper Martyn Margetson enjoyed a 15 year playing career with Manchester City, Southend United, Huddersfield Town and Cardiff City, among others.

Margetson became Cardiff's goalkeeper coach in 2005. The Wales national team goalkeeper coach was recommended to Sam Allardyce by the late Gary Speed, joining the Club in July 2011.

Attacking coach: Teddy Sheringham MBE

Born: 2 April 1966, Highams Park, England

A former England international forward, Teddy Sheringham enjoyed an outstanding career that saw him win three Premier League titles, the FA Cup and the UEFA Champions League with Manchester United.

A technically-gifted player, Sheringham spent three seasons with West Ham United between 2004-07, helping the Hammers to win the Championship Play-Offs in 2005.

Meet the Squad

West Ham United's first-team squad features players from all over the world, young and old, from full internationals to homegrown teenagers.

Regardless of their age, experience or background, all show the same pride and commitment whenever they pull on a Claret and Blue shirt. Over the next few pages, you can find out more about your heroes, from goalkeeper Adrian to centre forward Andy Carroll!

(All statistics correct to end of 2013/14 season)

ADRIAN

Born: 3 January 1987, Seville, Spain
Former clubs: Betis B, Real Betis
West Ham United: Appearances: 26   Goals: 0

Adrian San Miguel del Castillo – known simply as Adrian to supporters – is an imposing 6'3" shot-stopper who joined the Hammers in July 2013 following the expiration of his contract with hometown club Real Betis Balompie in Spain. Born and raised in Seville, Adrian enjoyed an outstanding breakthrough season in the Spanish top flight in 2012/13, keeping eleven clean sheets in 32 appearances.

After starting life as back-up to Jussi Jaaskelainen, Adrian's form saw him take over as West Ham United's No1 goalkeeper for the second half of the 2013/14 campaign. The Spaniard's passion on the pitch, amiable personality and enthusiastic use of social media, have made him a firm favourite among the Claret and Blue Army.

JUSSI JAASKELAINEN

Born: 19 April 1975, Mikkeli, Finland
Former clubs: Mikkelin Palloilijat, Vaasan Palloseura,
                    Bolton Wanderers
West Ham United: Appearances: 59   Goals: 0

A vastly experienced goalkeepeer, Jussi Jaaskelainen has enjoyed a fantastic career with Bolton Wanderers and West Ham United, with 2014/15 being his 18th season in English football.

Tall and athletic, Jaaskelainen initially moved to English football in 1997 for just £100,000 from his native Finland and became one of the biggest bargains in Premier League history by making more than 500 appearances for the Trotters. Jaaskelainen joined West Ham following the Club's promotion to the Premier League in 2012 and was rewarded for his consistent performances with a new one-year contract in summer 2014.

Athletic and the consummate professional, the former Finland international was also capped 56 times by his country.

CARL JENKINSON

Born: 8 February 1992, Harlow, Essex, England
Former clubs: Charlton Athletic, Arsenal
West Ham United: Appearances: 0   Goals: 0

Carl Jenkinson began his career at Charlton Athletic, where he enjoyed a fantastic 2010/11 season before being snapped up by Arsenal at the age of 19 in June 2011.

The right-back totalled 57 first-team appearances for the Gunners, appearing on 12 occasions in the UEFA Champions League and 37 times in the Premier League for Arsenal. After scoring his first goal in senior football for the Gunners in a 2-0 victory over Norwich City on the final day of the 2013/14 season, he was loaned to West Ham United in July 2014.

Capped at age-group level for Finland – the country of his mother's birth – Jenkinson committed his international future for England and made his debut for Roy Hodgson's side in a friendly defeat to Sweden in Stockholm that November.

WINSTON REID

Born: 3 July 1988, North Shore, New Zealand
Former clubs: SUB Sonderborg, FC Midtjylland
West Ham United: Appearances: 104   Goals: 6

A tall and powerful defender, Winston Reid started all three of New Zealand's matches at the 2010 FIFA World Cup in South Africa, scoring in the All Whites' 1-1 draw with Slovakia.

Centre-back Reid moved to Denmark at the age of ten, representing the Scandinavian nation at U19, U20 and U21 levels before switching international allegiance to the country of his birth in early 2010. After five years of first-team action at FC Midtjylland in Denmark, the 6'3 player moved to West Ham United in August 2010.

He starred as West Ham won promotion from the Championship in 2012 before earning the Hammer of the Year award following an outstanding 2012/13 campaign.

AARON CRESSWELL

Born: 15 December 1989, Liverpool, England
Former clubs: Tranmere Rovers, Ipswich Town
West Ham United: Appearances: 0   Goals: 0

Highly-rated left-back Aaron Cresswell joined the Hammers from Championship side Ipswich Town on a five-year contract in July 2014.

Born in Liverpool, Cresswell began his career with Tranmere Rovers before moving to Portman Road in 2011. He enjoyed three outstanding seasons with the Tractor Boys, making nearly 150 appearances and earning Player of the Year honours in 2012.

An outstanding 2013/14 season saw the attacking full-back voted into the Championship Team of the Year by his fellow professionals and earn a summer move to the Boleyn Ground.

JAMES TOMKINS

Born:	29 March 1989, Basildon, Essex
Former clubs:	Derby County (loan)
West Ham United:	Appearances: 186 Goals: 7

A centre-back, James Tomkins became a regular member of the West Ham United first team during the 2009/10 season, making more than 25 appearances. The ball-playing defender has been with the club since the age of seven and graduated from the Academy of football in 2007, making his first-team debut at Everton in March 2008.

Since then, Tomkins has established himself as a regular starter, playing his part as West Ham won promotion in 2012 and subsequently re-established themselves in the Premier League. Tomkins' ability has been recognised at international level, appearing at the 2009 and 2011 UEFA European U21 Championships with England and the London 2012 Olympic Games with Team GB.

JOEY O'BRIEN

Born:	17 February 1986, Dublin, Republic of Ireland
Former clubs:	Bolton Wanderers, Sheffield Wednesday (loan)
West Ham United:	Appearances: 87 Goals: 3

Republic of Ireland international Joey O'Brien joined West Ham United on a free transfer following a successful week-long trial in July 2011. A Premier League regular for Bolton Wanderers as a teenager, the Dubliner made his senior international debut just a week past his 20th birthday in March 2006.

Having suffered a disappointing three seasons fighting a succession of knee injuries, O'Brien proved his fitness to manager Sam Allardyce before being snapped up by the Hammers. Since his arrival, the Irishman has shown his value in a variety of defensive positions, becoming a favourite among the Boleyn Ground faithful for his whole-hearted displays.

JAMES COLLINS

Born:	23 August 1983, Newport, Wales
Former clubs:	Cardiff City, West Ham United, Aston Villa
West Ham United:	Appearances: 121 Goals: 5

A whole-hearted central defender, James Collins has represented his native Wales at every level. Now in his second spell at West Ham United after re-joining the club from Aston Villa on 1 August 2012, Collins began his career with Cardiff City before joining the Hammers in 2005

Known as 'Ginge' to all at the club, Collins helped West Ham to reach the 2006 FA Cup final and stave off relegation in dramatic style in 2007 before spending three years with Aston Villa between 2009 and 2012. Since his return, the Welshman has continued to impress his team-mates and supporters alike with his uncompromising and hugely effective defensive performances, while also weighing in with rare, yet valuable goals.

GUY DEMEL

Born:	13 June 1981, Orsay, France
Former clubs:	Nimes Olympique, Arsenal, Borussia Dortmund, Borussia Dortmund II, Hamburger SV
West Ham United:	Appearances: 75 Goals: 1

A versatile right-sided defender, Guy Demel has played professionally in France and Germany after spending a year with Arsenal early in his career. Capped more than 30 times by Ivory Coast, France-born Demel came through the ranks at Nimes Olympique before moving to Arsenal and subsequently enjoying success during a four-year spell with Borussia Dortmund.

A powerful yet skilful player, Demel established himself in the Ivory Coast national side during six seasons with Hamburger SV, where he featured regularly in European competition. A two-time FIFA World Cup finalist, Demel was part of the West Ham United side which won the 2012 Championship Play-Off final at Wembley.

DAN POTTS

Born:	13 April 1994, Barking, England
Former clubs:	Colchester United (loan), Portsmouth (loan)
West Ham United:	Appearances: 13 Goals: 0

A versatile and composed defender blessed with great ability, Dan Potts has followed his famous father Steve through the ranks at the Academy of Football.

Potts was rewarded with a first professional contract and first-team debut in the same week in December 2011, impressing as West Ham United scored a 1-0 home Npower Championship victory over Barnsley at the Boleyn Ground.

Already capped by England at U20 level, the teenager is looking to make his mark for both club and country over the coming years.

LEO CHAMBERS

Born:	5 August 1995, London, England
Former clubs:	None
West Ham United:	Appearances: 3 Goals: 0

Leo Chambers enjoyed a breakthrough season in 2013/14, making his first-team debut and featuring in Capital One Cup victories over Cheltenham Town, Cardiff City and Burnley. An intelligent defender who is comfortable at centre-back and right-back, Chambers has made his way up through the ranks at the Academy of Football and will hope to establish himself at first-team level in the future.

The youngster has long been considered one of West Ham United's brightest prospects and he certainly has the potential to go to the top. Further evidence is the fact that he has been capped regularly by England at age-group level in recent years.

KEVIN NOLAN

Born: 24 June 1982, Liverpool, England
Former clubs: Bolton Wanderers, Newcastle United
West Ham United: Appearances: 119 Goals: 30

A goalscoring midfielder, leader and inspirational figure, Kevin Nolan has enjoyed huge success with Bolton Wanderers and Newcastle United during his playing career. Born in Liverpool, Nolan spent a decade in the first-team squad at Bolton, scoring exactly 50 goals in 345 appearances and regularly being tipped for full international honours.

Nolan maintained his consistency during a two-and-a-half year spell at Newcastle, where he captained the Magpies to the Championship title in 2009/10. In his first season at the Boleyn Ground, the skipper led West Ham United to Npower Championship Play-Off final glory against Blackpool at Wembley in May 2012, and he has continued to lead from the front and hit the net regularly since then.

CHEIKHOU KOUYATE

Born: 21 December 1989, Dakar, Senegal
Former clubs: FC Brussels, Anderlecht, Kortrijk (loan)
West Ham United: Appearances: 0 Goals: 0

Cheikhou Kouyate joined West Ham United from Belgian giants Anderlecht in June 2014. Born in Dakar, Senegal, Kouyate moved to Belgium at the age of 15 and joined FC Brussels.

He earned a move to Anderlecht in the summer of 2008, quickly becoming a mainstay in the starting line-up. A first Belgian title arrived in the 2009/10 season, and he added to his medal collection as Anderlecht claimed the crown for the last three campaigns. In Europe, Kouyate played a full role as Anderlecht reached the knockout stages of the UEFA Europa League in 2009/10, 2010/11 and 2011/12, and the group phase of the UEFA Champions League for the last two seasons. Internationally, Kouyate represented his country at the 2012 London Olympic Games.

MATT JARVIS

Born: 22 May 1986, Middlesbrough, England
Former clubs: Gillingham, Wolverhampton Wanderers
West Ham United: Appearances: 69 Goals: 6

England international winger Matt Jarvis became West Ham United's club-record signing when he joined from Wolverhampton Wanderers in August 2012. After being released by Millwall as a youngster, Jarvis quickly became a star with Gillingham as a teenager before joining Wolves in June 2007.

The wideman made his mark in the Premier League with a number of eye-catching displays, earning his first senior England cap in a 1-1 friendly international draw with Ghana at Wembley in March 2011. Jarvis scored four times in 2013/14, including twice in the Hammers' run to the Capital One Cup quarter-finals in victories over Cardiff City and Tottenham Hotspur.

RICARDO VAZ TE

Born:	1 October 1986, Lisbon, Portugal
Former clubs:	Sporting Lisbon, SC Farense, Bolton Wanderers, Hull City (loan), Panionios, Hibernian, Barnsley
West Ham United:	Appearances: 56 Goals: 19

A tall, quick and powerful player, Ricardo Vaz Te is a versatile forward or winger who can both score and create goals for his team. Born in Portugal and raised in both his home nation and the African country of Guinea-Bissau, Vaz Te moved to English football at the age of 16 in 2003 when Sam Allardyce took him to Bolton Wanderers.

After making nearly 80 first-team appearances for the Trotters, Vaz Te played professionally in Greece and Scotland before returning to England with Barnsley in summer 2011. After six prolific months at Oakwell, he moved to the Boleyn Ground and scored the goal that took West Ham United back to the Premier League in the 2012 Championship Play-Off final victory over Blackpool at Wembley.

MARK NOBLE

Born:	8 May 1987, Canning Town, England
Former clubs:	Ipswich Town (loan), Hull City (loan)
West Ham United:	Appearances: 288 Goals: 33

Mark Noble is West Ham United's longest-serving player, having joined the Club as a full-time trainee in the summer of 2003. An experienced former England U21 midfielder, Noble was part of the Hammers' promotion from the Championship and 'Great Escape' from relegation from the Premier League in May 2007.

After scoring on his 100th appearance for the club at Blackburn Rovers in March 2009, Noble suffered relegation in 2011 before inspiring the Hammers back to the top flight the following year. That season, 2011/12, he was voted Hammer of the Year by his adoring fans, repeating that achievement at the end of the 2013/14 campaign.

RAVEL MORRISON

Born:	2 February 1993, Wythenshawe, Manchester, England
Former clubs:	Manchester United, Birmingham City (loan)
West Ham United:	Appearances: 22 Goals: 5

A talented attacking midfield player blessed with superb technique and passing ability, Ravel Morrison is considered to be one of English football's top young prospects. The Wythenshawe-born player joined Manchester United as a schoolboy before making his first-team debut at the age of 17 in October 2010.

Morrison moved to West Ham United in January 2012, making his debut as a substitute in the 1-1 Championship draw at Leeds United on 17 March of the same year. The England U21 international continued his development during a successful loan spell at Birmingham City during the 2012/13 season. In 2013/14, he made his name with a Goal of the Season winner at Tottenham Hotspur before being loaned to Queens Park Rangers, with whom he won promotion via the Championship Play-Off final.

MOHAMED DIAME

Born:	14 June 1987, Creteil, France
Former clubs:	RC Lens, CD Linares, Rayo Vallecano, Wigan Athletic
West Ham United:	Appearances: 75 Goals: 7

A strong and versatile player who predominantly operates from a central midfield position, Mohamed Diame is adaptability personified. Athletic, tall and as strong as any player in English football, Diame played professionally in France and Spain before making his name in this country during a successful spell with Wigan Athletic.

Capped regularly by Senegal in recent years, the French-born midfielder joined West Ham United on a three-year contract in June 2012, before captaining his country at the London 2012 Olympic Games later the same summer. Diame's first season in east London saw him win Signing, Goal and Individual Performance of the Season honours for his match-turning display in the 3-1 Premier League win over Chelsea at the Boleyn Ground.

STEWART DOWNING

Born:	22 July 1984, Middlesbrough, England
Former clubs:	Middlesbrough, Sunderland (loan), Aston Villa, Liverpool
West Ham United:	Appearances: 37 Goals: 1

Talented England international Stewart Downing joined West Ham United from Liverpool in August 2013 putting pen to paper on a four-year contract. The sight of the winger creating chances has delighted fans at Middlesbrough, Aston Villa and Liverpool, the latter of which benefited from a Man of the Match display by Downing as they won the Carling Cup in 2012.

Capped more than 30 times by his country, Downing travelled to the 2012 UEFA European Championship finals and won Player of the Year honours at all three clubs he represented on a permanent basis prior to his move to east London. The Middlesbrough-born player capped an encouraging debut season with the Hammers by scoring in the 2-0 home Premier League win over Tottenham Hotspur in May 2014.

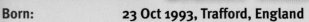

DANNY WHITEHEAD

Born:	23 Oct 1993, Trafford, England
Former clubs:	Stockport County
West Ham United:	Appearances: 1 Goals: 0

Manchester-born youngster Danny Whitehead was West Ham United's fourth summer signing of 2013, penning a two-year deal from Conference North outfit Stockport County. An attacking midfielder by trade, Whitehead joined the Hatters at the age of 14 and wasted no time making an impression, scoring regularly for their U18 side despite still being a schoolboy.

He subsequently made his first-team bow in September 2011 at just 17 years of age, coming off the bench in a 4-2 defeat by Fleetwood Town. His first goal for the club followed just a week later; with the youngster finding the net in a 2-2 stalemate away at Cambridge United. Whitehead turned out no fewer than 42 times for County in the 2012/13 campaign, scoring five times, prompting former Hatters manager Didi Hamann to recommend his services to West Ham.

A first-team debut for the Hammers arrived in January 2014, when he appeared in an FA Cup third-round defeat at Nottingham Forest.

DIEGO POYET

Born: 8 April 1995, Zaragoza, Spain
Former clubs: Charlton Athletic
West Ham United: Appearances: 0   Goals: 0

An industrious and tenacious midfielder blessed with an impressive range of passing, Poyet signed for Charlton Athletic as an eleven-year-old before coming through the Academy ranks at The Valley. The son of Sunderland manager Gus, Poyet burst into the Charlton first team in January 2014, making 23 impressive appearances during the second half of last season to earn the club's Player of the Year award. He joined West Ham United in July 2014.

ANDY CARROLL

Born: 6 January 1989, Gateshead, England
Former clubs: Newcastle United, Preston North End (loan), Liverpool
West Ham United: Appearances: 40   Goals: 9

England striker Andy Carroll initially joined West Ham United on loan from Liverpool in August 2012, making an eye-catching debut in a 3-0 home Premier League victory over Fulham two days later. After a successful debut campaign in east London, Carroll made his move permanent in a club-record deal in summer 2013.

Previously, the pony-tailed centre forward earned a fearsome reputation during his time at first club Newcastle United, where he helped fire the Magpies to promotion to the Premier League. A talismanic presence for club and country, Carroll scored in the 2012 FA Cup final for Liverpool and spearheaded England's attack at the 2012 UEFA European Championship finals, netting a trademark header in the 3-2 group-stage victory over Sweden.

MAURO ZARATE

Born: 18 March 1987, Haedo, Argentina
Former clubs: Velez Sarsfield, Al-Sadd, Birmingham City (loan), SS Lazio (loan), SS Lazio, Internazionale (loan), Velez Sarsfield
West Ham United: Appearances: 0   Goals: 0

Mauro Zarate became the Hammers' first summer capture of 2014 when he agreed to join the Club on a three-year contract with a further one-year option from Argentine side Velez Sarsfield.

Zarate arrived at the Boleyn Ground having enjoyed a prolific 2013/14 season in his homeland, where he finished as leading scorer in the Primera Division Torneo Final with 13 goals in 19 appearances, and 20 in 35 in all competitions.

A skilful attacker capable of playing in a centre forward or withdrawn role and scoring spectacular goals, the Haedo-born player also numbers Birmingham City and Italian giants Lazio and Internazionale among his former clubs.

ENNER VALENCIA

Born: 11 April 1989, San Lorenzo, Ecuador
Former clubs: Emelec, Pachuca
West Ham United: Appearances: 0   Goals: 0

Born in the port town of San Lorenzo on the north coast of Ecuador, close to the Colombian border, Enner Valencia began his career with Club Sport Emelec in the city of Guayaquil.

Valencia featured regularly in continental competition for Emelec before winning the Ecuadorian Serie A Championship Finals in 2013.

The striker joined Mexican club Pachuca in January 2014, banging in 18 goals in just 23 Torneo Clausura appearances before excelling for his country at the FIFA World Cup, where he scored three times.

ELLIOT LEE

Born: 16 December 1994, Newcastle-Upon-Tyne, England
Former clubs: Colchester United (loan)
West Ham United: Appearances: 2   Goals: 0

Stocky, powerful and blessed with a natural finisher's ability, Elliot Lee has been a prolific goalscorer at all age-group levels for West Ham United.

The son of former England midfielder Rob, Lee made his senior debut for the Hammers in an FA Cup third-round defeat at Manchester United in January 2013.

In August of the same year, a Barclays Premier League bow occurred in the home defeat by Stoke City before signing a new contract in summer 2014.

CARLTON COLE

Born: 12 October 1983, Croydon, England
Former clubs: Chelsea, Wolverhampton Wanderers (loan), Aston Villa (loan), Charlton Athletic (loan)
West Ham United: Appearances: 267   Goals: 65

Capped by England at full international level, Carlton Cole's career has flourished during his time at West Ham United, with the striker bagging the opening goal as the Hammers beat Blackpool 2-1 at Wembley in the 2012 Championship Play-Off final. A tall and powerful forward, Cole came through the ranks at Chelsea before finding his first-team opportunities limited by the arrival of a number of big-money signings at Stamford Bridge.

After scoring on his debut in August 2006, the likeable forward has enjoyed a long career in Claret and Blue, re-joining the Club in October 2013 after initially being released a few months earlier. A popular character on and off the pitch, Cole is heavily involved in charity and community work with a number of organisations.

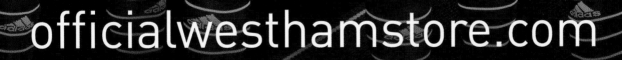
officialwesthamstore.com

stadium superstore	lakeside thurrock	liberty romford
Boleyn Ground,	Unit 71	Unit GLA1A (opposite Sports
Green Street,	Lakeside Shopping Centre,	Direct and next to Waterstones)
London E13 9AZ	RM20 2ZP	Liberty Shopping Centre

27

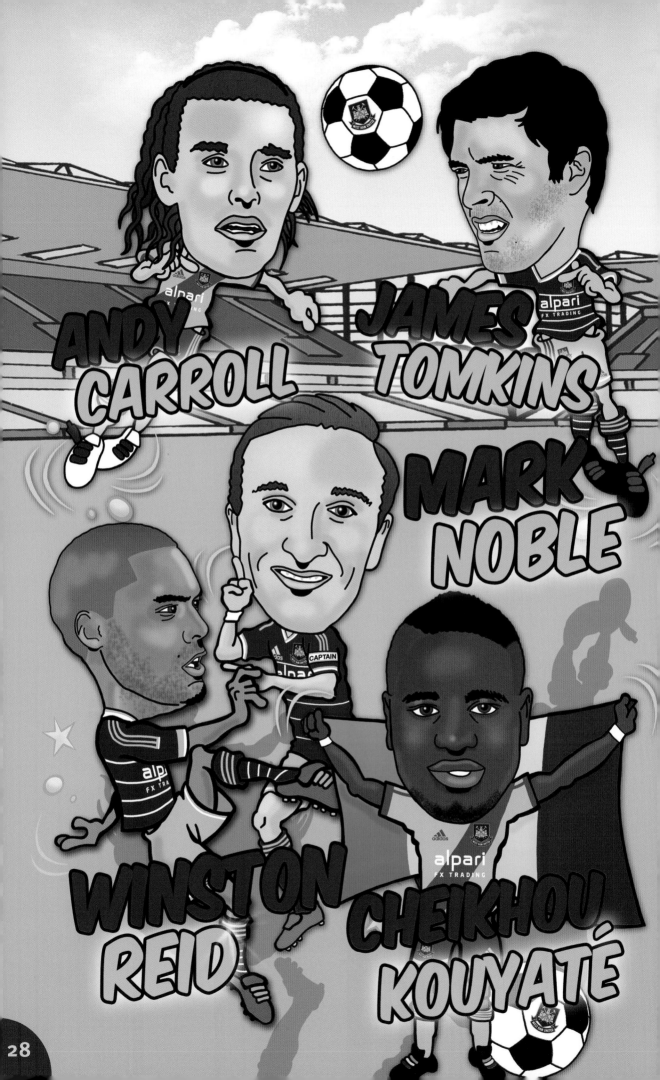

29

West Ham United
– by the Numbers

A numerical look back at the history of the Hammers

1 West Ham United have won one major European trophy, lifting the European Cup Winners' Cup by defeating German side TSV 1860 Munich 2-0 at Wembley on 19 May 1965.

2 West Ham United are one of only two teams to score three goals in an FA Cup final and lose. The Hammers drew 3-3 with Liverpool in 2006 before being beaten on penalties. Bolton Wanderers are the other side to do so, losing 4-3 to Blackpool in 1953.

3 West Ham United are one of three clubs to appear in two League Cup finals and lose them both. Bolton Wanderers and Everton are the other two.

4 West Ham United have played at four different stadia since the club's inception in 1895 – Hermit Road in Canning Town, Browning Road in East Ham, the Memorial Grounds in Plaistow and the Boleyn Ground in Upton Park.

5 West Ham United have been involved in three 5-5 draws in their history – at home to Aston Villa on 3 January 1931, at Newcastle United on 10 December 1960 and at Chelsea on 17 December 1966.

6 Bobby Moore's No6 shirt was retired in August 2008 to mark the 50th anniversary of the England great's West Ham United debut against Manchester United on 8 September 1958.

9 West Ham United's longest winning streak of league matches was the nine victories they recorded from 19 October-14 December 1985.

10 West Ham United hold the record for the joint-biggest victory in the League Cup. The Hammers defeated Bury 10-0 in the second round on 25 October 1983. That result was matched by Liverpool against Fulham, also in the second round, on 23 September 1986.

14 West Ham United have had 14 full-time managers in the Club's 112-year history.

14 West Ham United won a Club-record 14 away league matches during the 2011/12 season, which ended with promotion to the Barclays Premier League.

16 West Ham United won a club-record 16 home league matches in succession between 30 August 1980 and 7 March 1981.

19 West Ham United lost a club-record 19 consecutive away matches between 28 November 1959 and 15 October 1960.

27 West Ham United have gone 27 league matches without failing to score a goal on two occasions – between 22 January-15 October 1927 and between 5 October 1957-4 April 1958.

29 West Ham United conceded just 29 league goals during the 1980/81 Division Two promotion season, a club-record low.

38 Dylan Tombides' No38 was retired following his death at the age of 20 in April 2014, following a brave three-year battle with cancer.

50 Vic Watson scored 50 goals in all competitions in 1929/30, a Club record.

101 West Ham United scored a Club-record 101 goals in securing the Division Two title in 1957/58.

326 Vic Watson is West Ham United's all-time record goalscorer, netting 326 times in 505 appearances between 1920 and 1935.

708 John Lyall took charge of West Ham United 708 times between 1974 and 1989, more than any other manager in the Club's history.

793 Billy Bonds made a Club-record 793 first-team appearances for West Ham United between 1967 and 1988.

1895 The year Thames Ironworks FC – West Ham United's predecessor – was founded by Arnold Hills.

1900 West Ham United was officially inaugurated in June 1900, five years after the Club's predecessor, Thames Ironworks FC, had been founded.

44,232 West Ham United's record attendance, who attended the FA Cup sixth-round victory over Birmingham at the Boleyn Ground on 4 March 1933.

18,000,000

The largest transfer fee West Ham United **have ever received was the £18,000,000 Leeds United paid for England defender Rio Ferdinand in November 2000.**

West Ham United 2014/15

Back row (left to right):
Cheikhou Kouyate, James Collins, Kevin Nolan, Guy Demel, Carlton Cole, Jussi Jaaskelainen

Front row (left to right):
Matt Jarvis, Aaron Cresswell, Winston Reid, Mark Noble, Mohamed Diame

West Ham United

A concise look back on the history of the Hammers

WEST Ham United was founded in 1895 as Thames Ironworks FC before being reformed in 1900. In 1904 the Club relocated to their current Boleyn Ground stadium in Upton Park.

After initially competing in the Southern League and Western League, West Ham joined the Football League in 1919. Four years later, the Hammers celebrated the twin achievements of gaining promotion to Division One and reaching the first-ever Wembley FA Cup final, where they were beaten by Bolton Wanderers.

The 1920s and early 1930s were the domain of the Club's greatest-ever goalscorer, Vic Watson, who bagged an amazing 326 goals in Claret and Blue.

In 1940 the team returned to Wembley and won the inaugural Football League War Cup, defeating Blackburn Rovers at Wembley thanks to Sam Small's first-half winner.

West Ham won promotion to Division One for a second time in 1958, when victory at Middlesbrough secured the Division Two title on the final day of the season.

A few months later, a young Bobby Moore would make his debut against Manchester United – one of a host of fantastic home-grown players produced by what was fast becoming known around the world as the Academy of Football.

West Ham have continued to be regular visitors to the Home of Football, winning the FA Cup in 1964, 1975 and 1980 and the European Cup Winners' Cup in 1965, defeating German side TSV 1860 Munich 2-0 in the final.

The Hammers have also reached Wembley in the League Cup, holding Liverpool to a draw in 1981 before being beaten in a replay at Villa Park.

The Club finished as runners-up to West Bromwich Albion in the same competition in 1966 – the same year in which Moore, Geoff Hurst and Martin Peters led England to FIFA World Cup glory.

Moore captained the side, with Hurst netting a hat-trick and Peters the other goal in England's unforgettable 4-2 triumph over West Germany in the final at Wembley.

In continental competition, aside from their 1965 triumph, the Hammers reached the final of the European Cup Winners' Cup again in 1976, losing to Belgian club RSC Anderlecht, and won the UEFA Intertoto Cup in 1999.

In between, manager John Lyall guided West Ham to their third FA Cup win in 1980, when Trevor Brooking's header secured a shock 1-0 win for the Division Two Hammers over Arsenal.

A year later, West Ham raced to the Division Two title and promotion to the top-flight.

In terms of league position, West Ham's highest-ever finish was the third place achieved by Lyall's squad in 1985/86.

The Boys of '86 have since become heroes at the Boleyn Ground, with the likes of Tony Cottee, Frank McAvennie, Alvin Martin, Phil Parkes and Mark Ward considered to be among the Club's all-time greats.

West Ham were relegated in 2003 and 2011, but bounced back on both occasions via the Play-Offs.

In March 2013, the Club was named anchor tenant of the London 2012 Olympic Stadium, with the Hammers set to move into their new 54,000-capacity home in the summer of 2016.

HONOURS

European Cup Winners' Cup
Winners – 1965
Runners-up – 1976

FA Cup
Winners – 1964, 1975, 1980
Runners-up – 1923, 2006

League Cup
Runners-up – 1966, 1981

UEFA Intertoto Cup
Winners – 1999

Football League Championship
(Previously Division One and Division Two)
Winners – 1957/58, 1980/81
Runners-up – 1922/23, 1990/91, 1991/92

Football League Championship Play-Off
Winners – 2005, 2011
Runners-up – 2004

Football League War Cup
Winners – 1940

Charity Shield
Winners – 1964 (shared with Liverpool)

FA Youth Cup
Winners – 1963, 1981, 1999
Runners-up – 1957, 1959, 1975, 1996

Hammers Over The World

More than 100 overseas stars have played for West Ham United! How many can you name?

Clyde Best (Bermuda)

CANADA (2):
Alex Bunbury,
Craig Forrest

FRANCE (13):
Samassi Abou, Jeremie Aliadiere,
Christian Bassila, David Bellion,
Edouard Cisse, Laurent Courtois,
Alou Diarra, Julien Faubert,
Marc Keller, Bernard Lama,
Sebastien Schemmel,
Youssef Sofiane, David Terrier

BELGIUM (2):
Ruud Boffin,
Francois Van Der Els

SPAIN (4):
Adrian,
Manuel Almunia,
Kepa Blanco,
Diego Tristan

BERMUDA (1):
Clyde Best

UNITED STATES (4):
Ian Feuer,
John Harkes,
Sebatstian Lletget,
Jonathan Spector

PORTUGAL (6):
Paulo Alves,
Luis Boa Morte,
Dani Carvalho,
Paulo Futre,
Hugo Porfirio,
Ricardo Vaz Te

MEXICO (2):
Guillermo Franco,
Pablo Barrera

COLOMBIA (1):
Pablo Armero

PERU (1):
Nolberto Solano

SENEGAL (7):
Demba Ba,
Henri Camara,
Mohamed Diame,
Papa Bouba Diop,
Abdoulaye Faye,
Cheikhou Kouyate,
Diafra Sakho

CHILE (2):
Luis Jimenez,
Javier Margas

IVORY COAST (1)
Guy Demel

ARGENTINA (5):
Javier Mascherano,
Lionel Scaloni,
Mauricio Taricco,
Carlos Tevez,
Mauro Zarate

Carlos Tevez (Argentina)

AS one of the biggest clubs in the world, West Ham United have long scoured the globe for the very best talent.

In recent decades, football has become an increasingly global game. Therefore, it should come as no surprise that the Club has drawn players and staff from all over the planet.

Did you know that the Hammers have been represented by 128 players from 53 different countries outside the British Isles! So, how many of our foreign legion can you name?

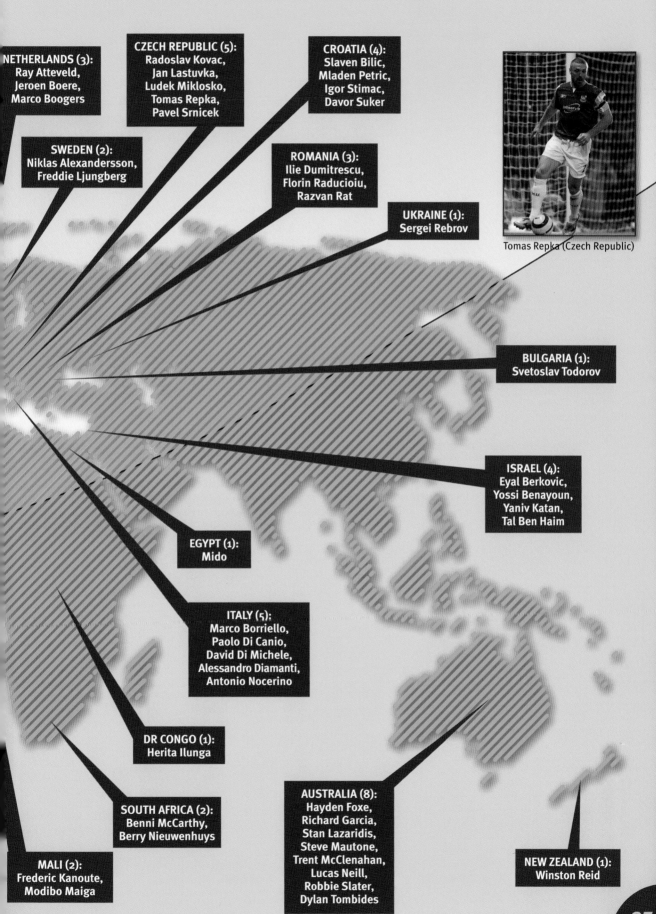

NETHERLANDS (3):
Ray Atteveld,
Jeroen Boere,
Marco Boogers

CZECH REPUBLIC (5):
Radoslav Kovac,
Jan Lastuvka,
Ludek Miklosko,
Tomas Repka,
Pavel Srnicek

CROATIA (4):
Slaven Bilic,
Mladen Petric,
Igor Stimac,
Davor Suker

SWEDEN (2):
Niklas Alexandersson,
Freddie Ljungberg

ROMANIA (3):
Ilie Dumitrescu,
Florin Raducioiu,
Razvan Rat

UKRAINE (1):
Sergei Rebrov

Tomas Repka (Czech Republic)

BULGARIA (1):
Svetoslav Todorov

ISRAEL (4):
Eyal Berkovic,
Yossi Benayoun,
Yaniv Katan,
Tal Ben Haim

EGYPT (1):
Mido

ITALY (5):
Marco Borriello,
Paolo Di Canio,
David Di Michele,
Alessandro Diamanti,
Antonio Nocerino

DR CONGO (1):
Herita Ilunga

SOUTH AFRICA (2):
Benni McCarthy,
Berry Nieuwenhuys

MALI (2):
Frederic Kanoute,
Modibo Maiga

AUSTRALIA (8):
Hayden Foxe,
Richard Garcia,
Stan Lazaridis,
Steve Mautone,
Trent McClenahan,
Lucas Neill,
Robbie Slater,
Dylan Tombides

NEW ZEALAND (1):
Winston Reid

Spot The Difference

Can you spot the ten differences between the two images of West Ham United being issued with a traditional Maori Haka challenge ahead of their Football United Tour meeting with Wellington Phoenix? Answers can be found on page 57!

38

officialwesthamstore.com

39

2013/14 Season Review

The 2013/14 season was one of highs and lows for West Ham United. Injuries and suspensions to important players left Sam Allardyce with a shortage of playing resources at times, but the Hammers battled through their difficulties to finish 13th in the Barclays Premier League table.

West Ham also won four ties to reach the Capital One Cup semi-finals, where they were beaten on aggregate by Barclays Premier League champions-elect Manchester City. Here, we take a photographic look back at a rollercoaster campaign.

AUGUST

Lifetime Achievement Award winner Billy Bonds MBE was honoured at the visit of Cardiff City

James Collins was voted Player of the Month for August

Joe Cole got the season up and running

Ricardo Vaz Te scored a fantastic free-kick against Cheltenham Town

Kevin Nolan's Chicken Dance made an early appearance!

West Ham United welcomed former player Frank O'Farrell back to the Boleyn Ground in August

SEPTEMBER

Jussi Jaaskelainen was in unbeatable form at Southampton

Mark Noble's joy turned to despair as the Hammers lost out to Everton

Sam Allardyce picked up some silverware at RCD Espanyol

Leo Chambers impressed in the Capital One Cup win over Cardiff City

Ravel Morrison was September's Player of the Month

The Boleyn Ground welcomed Dean Ashton in September

OCTOBER

Even the sprinklers were on West Ham United's side at White Hart Lane!

Matt Taylor was on target from the penalty spot at Burnley

Ravel Morrison was named Player of the Month for October

The players show their appreciation for the fans' support in north London

Supporter Paul Farrelle won an auction lot to be in West Ham United's team photo

There was plenty to celebrate during the 3-0 win over Fulham

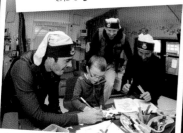
James Tomkins, James Collins and Razvan Rat spread some Christmas cheer at King George Hospital in Goodmayes

Joe Cole opened the scoring against West Bromwich Albion

The scoreboard only tells part of the story!

NOVEMBER

The mascots meet the players ahead of the visit of Chelsea

The players joined youngsters from Northbury Junior School in Barking for a spot of carol singing

West Ham United paid tribute to the fallen prior to the visit of Aston Villa

DECEMBER

The players paid a visit to Richard House Children's Hospice

The squad enjoyed a hearty Christmas dinner at Chadwell Heath

Ravel Morrison scored a wondergoal to complete an unforgettable win at Tottenham Hotspur

Adrian won January's Player of the Month award

JANUARY

Andy Carroll made a welcome return to action at Cardiff City

Hammers-supporting TV presenter Charlie Webster ran 250 miles for the Women's Aid charity

Marco Borriello and Antonio Nocerino joined the Hammers in January

Sam Allardyce had the last laugh against Jose Mourinho's Chelsea

There was plenty to celebrate following a goalless draw at Stamford Bridge

Marco Borriello played his part in the 2-0 victory at Villa Park

FEBRUARY

Sam Allardyce was the Barclays Manager of the Month following a perfect February

James Collins broke the deadlock late on against Norwich City

Antonio Nocerino enjoyed the vital win at Aston Villa

The old partnership combined to perfection against Swansea City

MARCH

Andy Carroll set West Ham United on their way to victory at Sunderland with a thumping header

Mark Noble was the Player of the Month for March

Sam Allardyce signs autographs for supporters before the home win over Hull City

Stewart Downing visited
Dycorts School in Romford

The goalscorer's kit awaits his
arrival at the Stadium of Light

Vice-Chairman Karren Brady received
her CBE at Buckingham Palace

APRIL

Alan Devonshire was given a warm
welcome on his return to the
Boleyn Ground

American football stars Andrew
Luck and Coby Fleener paid
West Ham United a visit

James Tomkins and George McCartney
met apprentices Mohamed Mohamed and
George Skuce at the Olympic Stadium

Flagbearers from West Ham United
Community Sports Trust added
colour to the Boleyn Ground

Matt Jarvis and Carlton Cole surveyed
West Ham United's new home in April

Unfortunately, Matt Jarvis' goal
at Arsenal was not enough to
stave off defeat

Guy Demel scored his maiden West Ham
United goal against Liverpool in April

West Ham United paid tribute to Dylan
Tombides at the visit of Crystal Palace

West Ham United supported the Kick
It Out anti-racism campaign at the
visit of Liverpool

Spaniard Adrian thanks the
fans for their support

MAY

The players paid tribute to
Dylan Tombides in their warm-up
for the visit of Spurs

Stewart Downing netted his first
goal for the Club in the 2-0
home win over Tottenham

The Italian Hammers were out
in numbers at the final home game
of the season

The season ended with a 2-0 defeat
by champions Manchester City

Cook Your Own East End Pie, Mash and Liquor!

NO trip to West Ham United is complete without a meal of traditional East End Pie, Mash and Liquor!

The origins of this world-famous dish can be traced back as far as the 18th century, when 'Pie and Mash Houses' emerged as a popular place to buy a cheap and plentiful meal. Back then, the pies were often filled with eels freshly caught in the nearby River Thames, due to their inexpensive price.

The dish continued to be developed in the East End and is still eaten today at a wide variety of traditional Pie and Mash Shops, some of which even offer a delivery service. The main dish today consists of pie, mash and liquor, with beef replacing eels in most cases. Liquor is green parsley gravy and is unique to pie and mash shops, who all claim to have their very own secret recipe.

Eels continue to be an east London speciality sold in pie and mash shops and are available in jellied or stewed form. The East End favourite is now enjoyed all over the country, so why not ask a responsible adult to help you to create your very own traditional West Ham United dinner!

INGREDIENTS

For the pie filling

- 1 tbsp olive oil
- 1 onion, chopped
- 2 cloves garlic, finely chopped
- 450g | 1lb minced beef steak or beef mince
- 1 tsp English mustard
- 1 tbsp tomato puree
- 1 beef stock cube
- vegetable oil
- 100ml | 3fl oz beef stock
- 2 tbsp plain flour
- salt and freshly ground black pepper

For the suet pastry

- 350g/12oz self-raising flour, plus extra for dusting
- 225g/8oz beef suet
- large knob of butter, softened, for greasing

For the pie crust

- 450g | 1lb ready-made shortcrust pastry, for the top of the pie
- 1 free-range egg yolk, lightly beaten

For the mashed potatoes

- 2 large potatoes - preferably Rooster or Nadine, peeled, cut into chunks
- 100ml | 3fl oz hot milk
- knob of butter

For the parsley liquor

- 50g | 2oz butter
- 50g | 2oz cornflour
- 500ml | 18fl oz chicken stock
- generous bunch of parsley, leaves only, chopped
- 1-2 garlic cloves, roasted and pureed, to taste

PREPARATION METHOD

1. For the filling, heat the olive oil in a large frying pan over a medium heat and fry the onion and garlic for five minutes or until softened. Add the mince and cook for five minutes, stirring occasionally, or until browned and cooked through.

2. Stir in the rest of the filling ingredients, season with salt and freshly ground black pepper and set aside to cool.

3. Preheat the oven to 180C/350F/Gas 4.

4. For the suet pastry, sift the flour into a mixing bowl with the suet and season with salt and freshly ground black pepper. Gradually mix in about four tablespoons of cold water, or until you have a moist but firm dough.

5. On a lightly floured work surface roll the dough out to a 2mm thickness.

6. Generously butter two individual pie dishes then line each with the suet pastry, so that it covers the base and sides completely. Divide the filling mixture between the two dishes.

7. For the pie crust, roll out the shortcrust pastry on a lightly floured work surface to a 2mm thickness and use it to cover the two pies, pushing down the edges to seal. Brush generously with the egg yolk and make a hole in the middle of the lid to allow steam to escape.

8. Place the pie dishes into a deep-sided roasting tin and pour in enough boiling water to come halfway up the sides of the pie dishes, taking care not to get any water on the pastry. Transfer to the oven and cook for 20-30 minutes, or until the pastry is crisp and golden and the filling steaming hot.

9. Meanwhile, for the mashed potatoes, steam (or boil) the potatoes for 20 minutes or until tender. Scald the milk then mash the potatoes with the hot milk, butter and plenty of salt and freshly ground black pepper until smooth.

10. For the parsley liquor, melt the butter in a saucepan over a medium heat and whisk in the cornflour to make a paste. Gradually stir in the stock, bring to a simmer, then stir in the parsley and garlic and stir until thickened and smooth.

11. Serve the hot pies with the mash and liquor.

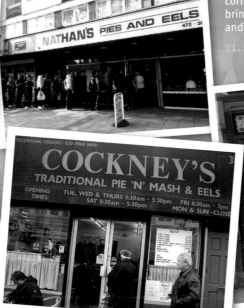

BUBBLES AND HAMMERHEAD'S 2015 ANNUAL TEASERS!

ANNUAL SPECIAL

CREATED BY ALEX BENNETT - WWW.FOOTBALLMISHMASH.COM

HI YOUTH ACADEMY MEMBERS! CAN YOU FIND THE NAMES OF OUR SQUAD IN THE GRID BELOW?

NAMES CAN GO UP, DOWN, DIAGONALLY AND BACKWARDS!

- AARON CRESSWELL
- ADRIAN
- AMOS NASHA
- ANDY CARROLL
- BLAIR TURGOTT
- CARLTON COLE
- CHEIKHOU KOUYATE
- DANIEL POTTS
- DANNY WHITEHEAD
- GUY DEMEL
- JAANAI GORDON
- JAMES COLLINS
- JAMES TOMKINS
- JOEY O'BRIEN
- JOSH CULLEN
- JUSSI JAASKELAINEN
- KEVIN NOLAN
- LEO CHAMBERS
- MOHAMED DIAME
- PAUL McCALLUM
- RAPHAEL SPIEGEL
- RAVEL MORRISON
- REECE BURKE
- RICARDO VAZ TE
- SEAN MAGUIRE
- SEBASTIAN LLETGET
- STEPHEN HENDERSON
- DIEGO POYET
- ELLIOT LEE
- ENNER VALENCIA
- GEORGE MONCUR
- MARK NOBLE
- MATTHIAS FANIMO
- MAURO ZARATE
- MODIBO MAIGA
- STEWART DOWNING
- WINSTON REID

A special look back through the West Ham United memorabilia archive

WEST Ham United memorabilia collector Steve Marsh has a house full of Hammers-related goodies. In a special edition of his popular Official Programme column, Marsh brings young readers a taste of how football used to be! On these pages, you will learn all about the history of the Fantasy Football craze and the amazing story of the FA Cup final song!

FANTASY FOOTBALL FEVER

NOWADAYS, you play fantasy football online, with would-be managers picking their imaginary teams at the click of a mouse. Twenty years ago, though, it was a game played in newspapers and magazines. To pick your team, you had to write it onto a form, cut it out and send it off in the post!

The craze originally gripped the nation at the beginning of the 1990s. The original concept was created by Englishman Andrew Wainstein. Fantasy football is a game in which participants assemble an imaginary team of real-life footballers and score points based on those players' actual statistical performance or their perceived contribution on the field of play.

Comedians David Baddiel and Frank Skinner brought the popular newspaper game to television screens in their programme 'Fantasy Football League', which was first aired in January 1994.

The format of the show was reliant on an actual fantasy football league, made up of teams picked by guest celebrities. A year later Baddiel and Skinner brought out a board game version by Playtime Games. Twelve player game cards were issued for each of the 20 Premiership teams for the 1994/95 season.

Players take the role of football manager and receive an initial fund of £25million to assemble a squad of players. The combined West Ham United's squad valued at that time totalled £10million.

The cards shown here feature three West Ham United players of the day – goalkeeper Ludek Miklosko, defender Tony Gale and midfielder Mike Marsh.

What price the Hammers squad today? The game cards, however, can be snapped up for a mere 25 pence each.

THE FA CUP FINAL SONG

OVER the years, football and music have gone arm in arm, especially when it comes to the FA Cup final.

Traditionally, since the 1927 FA Cup Final at Wembley between Arsenal and Cardiff City, the first and last verses of the hymn 'Abide with Me' has been sung before kick-off.

However, one of the other more recent quaint traditions that has unfortunately faded and died in recent years has been that of the official FA Cup final song performed by squad players from both competing sides, usually consisting of footballers with oversized headphones singing awkwardly.

The Hammers' 1975 FA Cup final squad's rendition of 'I'm Forever Blowing Bubbles' stayed in the charts for two weeks and reached the heady heights of number 31, whereas Fulham's 'El Viva El Fulham' sung by Tony Rees and the Cottagers to the tune of 'Y Viva Espana' peaked at number 46.

Other FA Cup final classics include Chelsea's 'Blue is the Colour' in 1972 and Tottenham Hotspur's 'Ossie's Dream' sung by Chas 'n' Dave in 1981. Both reached number 5.

Finally, former West Ham manager Alan Pardew belted out 'Glad All Over' for Crystal Palace in 1990, reaching number 50 in the UK charts!

Academy Aces

These five promising young players all hope to be West Ham United's next big thing!

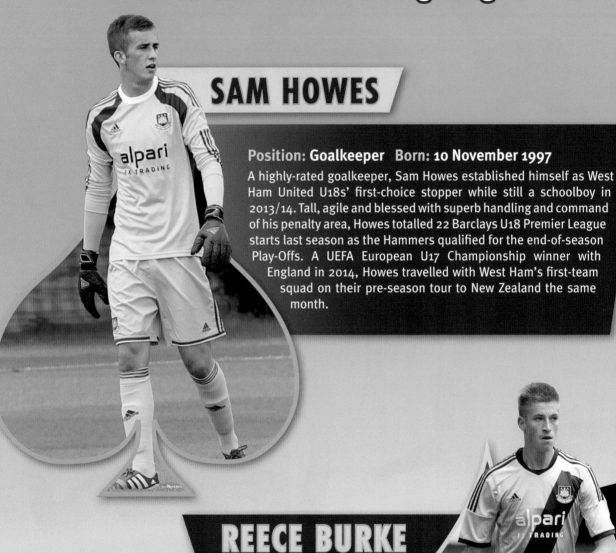

SAM HOWES

Position: Goalkeeper   **Born:** 10 November 1997

A highly-rated goalkeeper, Sam Howes established himself as West Ham United U18s' first-choice stopper while still a schoolboy in 2013/14. Tall, agile and blessed with superb handling and command of his penalty area, Howes totalled 22 Barclays U18 Premier League starts last season as the Hammers qualified for the end-of-season Play-Offs. A UEFA European U17 Championship winner with England in 2014, Howes travelled with West Ham's first-team squad on their pre-season tour to New Zealand the same month.

REECE BURKE

Position: Defender   **Born:** 2 September 1996

Tall, athletic and composed with the ball at his feet, Reece Burke came to the attention of West Ham United supporters when he bagged the late winner in the 3-2 pre-season win over UC Sampdoria in August 2014. Prior to that, the 18-year-old was handed his competitive senior debut in the FA Cup third-round defeat at Nottingham Forest in January 2014. Burke was also given an opportunity to shine for the first team during the Schalke 04 Cup in Germany and did not look out of place at all.

JOSH CULLEN

Position: Midfielder   Born: 7 April 1996

Eighteen-year-old central midfielder Josh Cullen is considered to be one of the brightest prospects to have emerged from the Academy of Football in recent seasons. An energetic, all-action player blessed with tenacious tackling ability and technical skills, Cullen won the Dylan Tombides Award for the Academy's outstanding player for 2013/14. Capped by England at U16 level, Cullen switched his international allegiance to Republic of Ireland in 2014, making his debut for the country's U18s in April 2014.

REECE OXFORD

Position: Centre-back   Born: 16 December 1998

Central defender Reece Oxford began the 2014/15 season as a schoolboy within the West Ham United Academy, but there is no doubt that the 15-year-old is developing quickly. Tall, strong, comfortable in possession and a fine reader of the game, the teenager captained England U17s twice at the Nordic Tournament in Denmark in the summer and has high hopes of continuing his international career. Such is Oxford's potential that he made his debut for the Hammers' U18 side just a month past his 15th birthday in a Barclays U18 Premier League win over Norwich City in January 2014.

JORDAN BROWN

Position: Striker   Born: 10 November 1996

A strong and athletic striker, Jordan Brown joined West Ham United from cross-London rivals Arsenal as a first-year scholar in July 2013. Capped seven times by England at U16 level, scoring three goals, Brown made eleven youth-team appearances for the Gunners while still a schoolboy. After netting 12 times in the Barclays U18 Premier League in 2013/14, the teenager started the current season in prolific form for the Hammers.

New Zealand 2014

West Ham United travelled 11,400 miles to New Zealand for the pre-season Football United Tour

WEST Ham United travelled further than ever when they headed to New Zealand in summer 2014.

The Hammers spent ten days on the other side of the world, meeting thousands of fans and contesting two matches during an unforgettable Football United Tour.

Hosted by the A-League club Wellington Phoenix, the tournament was a week-long festival of football which also involved Australian club Sydney FC and Barclays Premier League side Newcastle United.

On arrival, the squad and staff received a traditional Maori welcome, including a Hongi nose-rubbing ceremony that involved All Whites captain Winston Reid, Joint-Chairman David Gold, manager Sam Allardyce and Hammer of the Year Mark Noble.

The Claret and Blue Army descended on New Zealand from all over the planet, while the Hammers also made plenty of new friends during open training sessions at Auckland's North Harbour Stadium and Eden Park and Wellington's Westpac Stadium.

The sessions were also attended by local sporting superstars in the shape of the All Blacks rugby union team, while the players also used their free time to get out and see the sights of New Zealand's two largest cities.

The highlight of the trip for many players was a visit to the Weta Workshop and Park Road Post Production studios in the Wellington suburb of Miramar, where they got to grips with props from films like The Hobbit and Lord of the Rings and met Oscar-winning sound engineer Michael Hedges.

Unfortunately, the matches themselves did not go to plan, with Wellington Phoenix winning 3-1 at Eden Park and Sydney FC running out 2-1 winners at Westpac Stadium.

The pre-season also saw West Ham draw 2-2 and 0-0 at Stevenage and Ipswich Town respectively, beat German side Schalke 04 on penalties and lose 2-0 to Spanish outfit Malaga in Gelsenkirchen and defeat Italian club UC Sampdoria 3-2 at the Boleyn Ground.

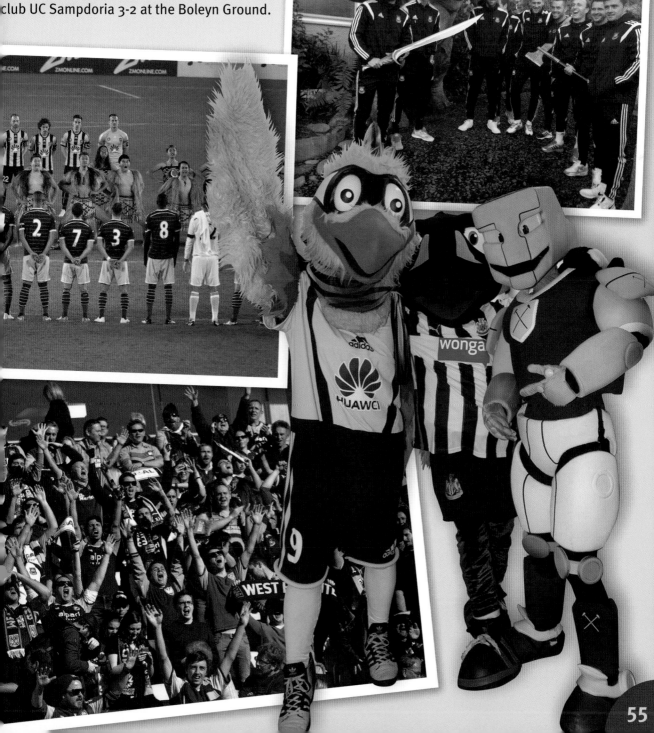

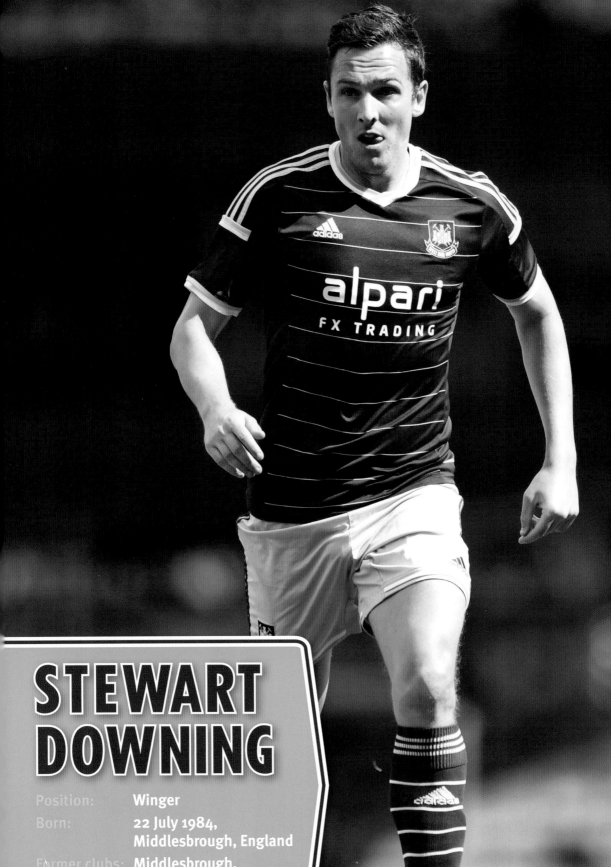

STEWART DOWNING

Position: **Winger**

Born: **22 July 1984, Middlesbrough, England**

Former clubs: **Middlesbrough, Sunderland (loan), Aston Villa, Liverpool**

57

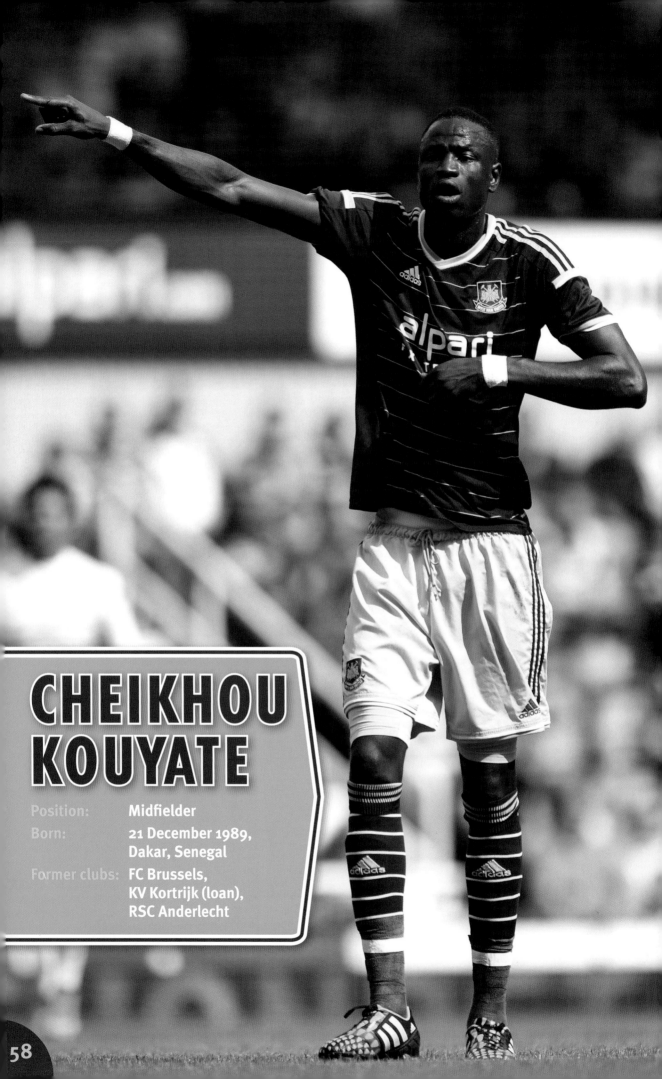

CHEIKHOU KOUYATE

Position: **Midfielder**

Born: **21 December 1989, Dakar, Senegal**

Former clubs: **FC Brussels, KV Kortrijk (loan), RSC Anderlecht**

2015 West Ham United
Birthday Calendar

Do you share a birthday with any of your Hammers heroes?

17 February

JANUARY

3   Adrian (28)
6   Andy Carroll (26)
28   Matthias Fanimo (21)

29 March

FEBRUARY

2   Ravel Morrison (22)
4   Sam Westley (21)
5   David Sullivan (66)
8   Carl Jenkinson (23)
17   Joey O'Brien (29)

MARCH

18   Mauro Zarate (28)
29   James Tomkins (26)

APRIL

2   Teddy Sheringham (49)
8   Diego Poyet (20)
11   Enner Valencia (26)
13   Dan Potts (21)
19   Jussi Jaaskelainen (40)

8 April

MAY

1   Sean Maguire (21)
8   Mark Noble (28)
22   Matt Jarvis (29)
22   Blair Turgott (21)

19 April

8 May

JUNE

13 Guy Demel (34)
14 Mohamed Diame (28)
24 Kevin Nolan (33)

24 June

JULY

3 Winston Reid (27)
28 Paul McCallum (22)

3 July

AUGUST

5 Leo Chambers (20)
18 George Moncur (22)
23 James Collins (32)

SEPTEMBER

3 Sebastian Lletget (23)
8 Martyn Margetson (44)
9 David Gold (79)
14 Kieran Sadlier (21)

OCTOBER

1 Ricardo Vaz Te (29)
19 Sam Allardyce (61)
23 Danny Whitehead (22)

NOVEMBER

2 Neil McDonald (50)

1 October

DECEMBER

5 Ian Hendon (44)
15 Aaron Cresswell (26)
16 Elliot Lee (21)
19 Raphael Spiegel (23)
21 Cheikhou Kouyate (26)

19 April

Spot The Difference Solution

Did you spot all of the ten differences between the two images of West Ham United being issued with a traditional Maori Haka challenge ahead of their Football United Tour meeting with Wellington Phoenix?